The Key Facts™

on

Saudi Arabia

Essential Information on Saudi Arabia

By Patrick W. Nee

The Internationalist®

www.internationalist.com

The Internationalist®

International Business, Investment, and Travel

Published by:

The Internationalist Publishing Company

96 Walter Street/ Suite 200

Boston, MA 02131, USA

Tel: 617-354-7722

www.internationalist.com

PN@internationalist.com

Table Of Contents

Chapter 1: Background

Saudi Arabia is the birthplace of Islam and home to Islam's two holiest shrines in Mecca and Medina. The king's official title is the Custodian of the Two Holy Mosques. The modern Saudi state was founded in 1932 by ABD AL-AZIZ bin Abd al-Rahman Al SAUD (Ibn Saud) after a 30-year campaign to unify most of the Arabian Peninsula. One of his male descendents rules the country today as required by the country's 1992 Basic Law. King SALMAN bin Abd al-Aziz ascended to the throne in 2015 and placed the first next-generation prince, MUHAMMAD BIN NAYIF bin Abd al-Aziz, in the line of succession as Crown Prince. Following Iraq's invasion of Kuwait in 1990, Saudi Arabia accepted the Kuwaiti royal family and 400,000 refugees while allowing Western and Arab troops to deploy on its soil for the liberation of Kuwait the following year. The continuing presence of foreign troops on Saudi soil after the liberation of Kuwait became a source of tension between the royal family and the public until all operational US troops left the country in 2003.

Major terrorist attacks in May and November 2003 spurred a strong on-going campaign against domestic terrorism and extremism. King ABDALLAH from 2005 to 2015 worked to incrementally modernize the Kingdom – driven by personal ideology and political pragmatism – through a series of social and economic initiatives, including expanding employment and social opportunities for women, attracting foreign investment increasing the role of the private sector in the economy, and discouraging businesses from hiring foreign workers. The Arab Spring inspired protests – increasing in number since 2011 but usually small in size – over primarily domestic issues among Saudi Arabia's majority Sunni population. Riyadh has taken a cautious but firm approach by arresting some protesters but releasing most of them quickly, and by using its state-sponsored clerics to counter political and Islamist activism. In addition, Saudi Arabia has seen protests among the Shia populace in the eastern Province, who have protested primarily against the detention of political prisoners, endemic discrimination, and

Bahraini and Saudi Government actions in Bahrain. Protests are met by a strong police presence, with some arrests, but not the level of bloodshed seen in protests elsewhere in the region. In response to the unrest, King ABDALLAH in February and March 2011 announced a series of benefits to Saudi citizens including funds to build affordable housing, salary increases for government workers, and unemployment entitlements. To promote increased political participation, the government held elections nationwide in September 2011 for half the members of 285 municipal councils – a body that holds little influence in the Saudi Government. Also in September, the king announced that women will be allowed to run for and vote in future municipal elections - first held in 2005 - and serve as full members of the advisory Consultative Council. The country remains a leading producer of oil and natural gas and holds more than 16% of the world's proven oil reserves. The government continues to pursue economic reform and diversification, particularly since Saudi Arabia's accession to the

WTO in December 2005, and promotes foreign investment in the kingdom. A burgeoning population, aquifer depletion, and an economy largely dependent on petroleum output and prices are all ongoing governmental concerns.

Chapter 2: Geography

Location:

Middle East, bordering the Persian Gulf and the Red Sea, north of Yemen

Geographic coordinates:

25 00 N, 45 00 E

Map references:

Middle East

Area:

total: 2,149,690 sq km

country comparison to the world: 13

land: 2,149,690 sq km

water: 0 sq km

Area - comparative:

slightly more than one-fifth the size of the US

Land boundaries:

total: 4,272 km

border countries: Iraq 811 km, Jordan 731 km, Kuwait 221 km, Oman 658 km, Qatar 87 km, UAE 457 km, Yemen 1,307 km

Coastline:

2,640 km

Maritime claims:

territorial sea: 12 nm

contiguous zone: 18 nm

continental shelf: not specified

Climate:

harsh, dry desert with great temperature extremes

Terrain:

mostly uninhabited, sandy desert

Elevation extremes:

lowest point: Persian Gulf 0 m

highest point: Jabal Sawda' 3,133 m

Natural resources:

petroleum, natural gas, iron ore, gold, copper

Land use:

arable land: 1.47%

permanent crops: 0.11%

other: 98.42% (2005)

Irrigated land:

16,200 sq km (2004)

Total renewable water resources:

2.4 cu km (2011)

Freshwater withdrawal (domestic/industrial/agricultural):

total: 23.67 cu km/yr (9%/3%/88%)

per capita: 928.1 cu m/yr (2006)

Natural hazards:

frequent sand and dust storms

volcanism: despite many volcanic formations, there has been little activity in the past few centuries; volcanoes include Harrat Rahat, Harrat Khaybar, Harrat Lunayyir, and Jabal Yar

Environment - current issues:

desertification; depletion of underground water resources; the lack of perennial rivers or permanent water bodies has prompted the development of extensive seawater desalination facilities; coastal pollution from oil spills

Environment - international agreements:

party to: Biodiversity, Climate Change, Climate Change-Kyoto Protocol, Desertification, Endangered Species, Hazardous Wastes, Law of the Sea, Marine Dumping, Ozone Layer Protection, Ship Pollution

signed, but not ratified: none of the selected agreements

Geography - note:

Saudi Arabia is the largest country in the world without a river; extensive coastlines on the Persian Gulf and Red Sea provide great leverage on shipping (especially crude oil) through the Persian Gulf and Suez Canal

Chapter 3: People and Society

Nationality:

noun: Saudi(s)

adjective: Saudi or Saudi Arabian

Ethnic groups:

Arab 90%, Afro-Asian 10%

Languages:

Arabic (official)

Religions:

Muslim (official; citizens are 85-90% Sunni and 10-15% Shia), other (includes Eastern orthodox, Protestant, Roman Catholic, Jewish, Hindu, Buddhist, and Sikh) (2012 est.)

note: despite having a large expatriate community of various faiths (more than 30% of the population), most forms of public religious expression inconsistent with the government-sanctioned interpretation of Sunni Islam are restricted; non-Muslims are not allowed to have Saudi citizenship and non-Muslim places of worship are not permitted (2013)

Population:

27,345,986 (July 2014 est.)

country comparison to the world: 47

note: immigrants make up more than 30% of the total population, according ot UN data

Age structure:

0-14 years: 27.6% (male 3,869,961/female 3,681,616)

15-24 years: 19.3% (male 2,832,538/female 2,458,339)

25-54 years: 45.4% (male 7,086,004/female 5,323,373)

55-64 years: 4.5% (male 674,571/female 555,136)

65 years and over: 3.2% (male 444,302/female 420,146) (2014 est.)

Median age:

total: 26.4 years

male: 27.3 years

female: 25.3 years (2014 est.)

Population growth rate:

1.49% (2014 est.)

country comparison to the world: 81

Birth rate:

18.78 births/1,000 population (2014 est.)

country comparison to the world: 96

Death rate:

3.32 deaths/1,000 population (2014 est.)

country comparison to the world: 219

Net migration rate:

-0.59 migrant(s)/1,000 population (2014 est.)

country comparison to the world: 138

Urbanization:

urban population: 82.9% of total population (2014)

rate of urbanization: 2.1% annual rate of change (2010-15 est.)

Major cities - population:

RIYADH (capital) 6.195 million; Jeddah 3.988 million; Mecca 1.742 million; Medina 1.258 million; Ad Dammam 1.043 million (2014)

Sex ratio:

at birth: 1.05 male(s)/female

under 15 years: 1.05 male(s)/female

15-64 years: 1.29 male(s)/female

65 years and over: 1.08 male(s)/female

total population: 1.21 male(s)/female (2014 est.)

Maternal mortality rate:

16 deaths/100,000 live births (2013)

country comparison to the world: 133

Infant mortality rate:

total: 14.58 deaths/1,000 live births

country comparison to the world: 110

male: 16.73 deaths/1,000 live births

female: 12.32 deaths/1,000 live births (2014 est.)

Life expectancy at birth:

total population: 74.82 years

country comparison to the world: 108

male: 72.79 years

female: 76.94 years (2014 est.)

Total fertility rate:

2.17 children born/woman (2014 est.)

country comparison to the world: 104

Health expenditures:

3.2% of GDP (2012)

country comparison to the world: 178

Physicians density:

0.77 physicians/1,000 population (2009)

Hospital bed density:

2.1 beds/1,000 population (2012)

HIV/AIDS - adult prevalence rate:

NA

HIV/AIDS - people living with HIV/AIDS:

NA

HIV/AIDS - deaths:

NA

Obesity - adult prevalence rate:

33% (2008)

country comparison to the world: 19

Children under the age of 5 years underweight:

5.3% (2005)

country comparison to the world: 88

Education expenditures:

5.1% of GDP (2008)

country comparison to the world: 68

Literacy:

definition: age 15 and over can read and write

total population: 94.4%

male: 96.5%

female: 91.4% (2013 est.)

School life expectancy (primary to tertiary education):

total: 16 years

male: 15 years

female: 16 years (2012)

Unemployment, youth ages 15-24:

> total: 28.3%
>
> country comparison to the world: 29
>
> male: 20.8%
>
> female: 54.4% (2012 est.)

Chapter 4: Government

Country name:

conventional long form: Kingdom of Saudi
Arabia

conventional short form: Saudi Arabia

local long form: Al Mamlakah al Arabiyah as
Suudiyah

local short form: Al Arabiyah as Suudiyah

Government type:

monarchy

Capital:

name: Riyadh

geographic coordinates: 24 39 N, 46 42 E

time difference: UTC+3 (8 hours ahead of
Washington, DC during Standard Time)

Administrative divisions:

13 provinces (mintaqat, singular - mintaqah); Al
Bahah, Al Hudud ash Shamaliyah (Northern
Border), Al Jawf, Al Madinah (Medina), Al
Qasim, Ar Riyad (Riyadh), Ash Sharqiyah
(Eastern), 'Asir, Ha'il, Jizan, Makkah (Mecca),
Najran, Tabuk

Independence:

23 September 1932 (unification of the kingdom)

National holiday:

Unification of the Kingdom, 23 September (1932)

Constitution:

1 March 1992 – basic Law of Government, issued by royal decree, serves as the constitutional framework and is based on the Qur'an and the life and tradition of the Prophet Muhammad (2013)

Legal system:

Islamic (sharia) legal system with some elements of Egyptian, French, and customary law; note - several secular codes have been introduced; commercial disputes handled by special committees

International law organization participation:

has not submitted an ICJ jurisdiction declaration; non-party state to the ICCt

Suffrage:

21 years of age; male

Executive branch:

<u>chief of state</u>: King and Prime Minister SALMAN bin Abd al-Aziz Al Saud (since 23 January 2015); Heir Apparent Crown Prince

MUQRIN bin Abd al-Aziz Al Saud (born 15
September 1945) ; Heir to the Crown Prince
MUHAMMAD BIN NAYIF bin Abd al-Aziz Al
Saud (born 30 August 1959); note – the monarch
is both chief of state and head of government

head of government: King and Prime Minister
SALMAN bin Abd al-Aziz Al Saud (since 23
January 2015); Deputy Prime Minister
MUQRIN bin Abd al-Aziz Al Saud (since 23
January 2015); Second Deputy Prime Minister
MUHAMMAD BIN NAYIF bin Abd al-Aziz Al
Saud (since 23 January 2015)

cabinet: Council of Ministers appointed by the
monarch every four years and includes many
royal family members

elections: none; the monarchy is hereditary; note
– an Allegiance Commission created by royal
decree in October 2006 established a committee
of Saudi princes that will play a role in selecting
future Saudi Kings

Legislative branch:

description: unicameral Consultative Council or
Majlis al-Shura (150 seats; members appointed
by the monarch to serve 4-year terms); note – in

early 2013, the monarch granted women 30 seats on the Council

Judicial branch:

highest court(s): High Court (consists of the court chief and organized into circuits with 3-judge panels except the criminal circuit which has a 5-judge panel for cases involving major punishments)

juge selection and term of office: the High Court chief and chiefs of the High Court Circuits appointed by royal decree folowing the recommendation of the Supreme Judiciary Council, a 10-member body of high level judges and other judicial heads; new judges and assistant judges serve 1- and 2-year probations, respectively, before permanent assignment

subordinate courts: Court of Appeals; first-degree courts composed of general, criminal, personal status, and commercial courts, and the Labor Court; hierarchy of administrative courts

note: in 2005, King Abdullah issued decrees approving an overhaul of the judicial system and which were incorporated in the Judiciary Law of 2007; changes include the establishment of a

High court and special commercial, labor, and administrative courts

Political parties and leaders:

Political pressure groups and leaders:

other: gas companies; religious groups

International organization participation:

ABEDA, AfDB (nonregional member), AFESD, AMF, BIS, CAEU, CP, FAO, G-20, G-77, GCC, IAEA, IBRD, ICAO, ICC (national committees), ICRM, IDA, IDB, IFAD, IFC, IFRCS, IHO, ILO, IMF, IMO, IMSO, Interpol, IOC, IOM (observer), IPU, ISO, ITSO, ITU, LAS, MIGA, NAM, OAPEC, OAS (observer), OIC, OPCW, OPEC, PCA, UN, UNCTAD, UNESCO, UNIDO, UNRWA, UNWTO, UPU, WCO, WFTU (NGOs), WHO, WIPO, WMO, WTO

Diplomatic representation in the US:

chief of mission: Ambassador Adil al-Ahmad al-JUBAYR (since 21 February 2007)

chancery: 601 New Hampshire Avenue NW, Washington, DC 20037

telephone: [1] (202) 342-3800

FAX: [1] (202) 944-3113

consulate(s) general: Houston, Los Angeles, New York

Diplomatic representation from the US:

chief of mission: Ambassador Joseph William WESTPHAL (since 26 March 2014)

embassy: Collector Road M, Diplomatic Quarter, Riyadh

mailing address: American Embassy, Unit 61307, APO AE 09803-1307; International Mail: P. O. Box 94309, Riyadh 11693

telephone: [966] (1) 488-3800

FAX: [966] (1) 488-7360

consulate(s) general: Dhahran, Jiddah (Jeddah)

King	**SALMAN bin Abd al-Aziz Al Saud**
Prime Min.	**SALMAN bin Abd al-Aziz Al Saud**
Dep. Prime Min.	**MUQRIN bin Abd al-Aziz Al Saud**

Second Dep. Prime Min.	**MUHAMMAD BIN NAYIF bin Abd al-Aziz Al Saud**
Min. of Agriculture	**Abd al-rahman bin Abd al-Muhsin al-FADHLI**
Min. of Civil Service	**Khalid bin Abdallah al-ARAJ**
Min. of Commerce & Industry	**Tawfiq bin Fawzan al-RABIAH**
Min. of Communications & Information Technology	**Muhammad bin Ibrahim al-SUWAYL**
Min. of Culture & Information	**Adil bin Zayid al-TURAYFI**
Min. of Defense	**MUHAMMAD BIN SALMAN**

	bin Abd al-Aziz Al Saud
Min. of Economy & Planning	**Muhammad bin Sulayman al-JASIR**
Min. of Education	**Azzam bin Muhammad al-DAKHIL**
Min. of Finance	**Ibrahim Abd al-Aziz al-ASSAF**
Min. of Foreign Affairs	**SAUD al-Faysal bin Abd al-Aziz Al Saud**
Min. of Health	**Ahmad bin Aqil al-KHATIB**
Min. of Housing	**Shawaysh bin Saud al-DHUWAYHI**
Min. of Interior	**MUHAMMAD bin Nayif bin Abd al-Aziz Al Saud**

Min. for Islamic Affairs, Endowment, Call, & Guidance	**Salih bin Abd al-Aziz bin Muhammad bin Ibrahim AL al-SHAYKH**
Min. of Justice	**Walid al-SAMANI**
Min. of Labor	**Adil bin Muhammad bin Abd al-Qadir FAQIYAH**
Min. of Municipal & Rural Affairs	**Abd al-Latif bin abd al-Malik bin Omar AL AL-SHAYKH**
Min. of Petroleum & Mineral Resources	**Ali Ibrahim al-NAIMI**
Min. of Pilgrimage Affairs & Religious Trusts	**Bandar bin Muhammad HAJJAR**
Min. of Social	**Majid bin**

Affairs	**Abdallah al-QASABI**
Min. of Transport	**Abdallah bin Abd al-Rahman al-MUQBIL**
Min. of Water & Electricity	**Abdallah bin Abd al-Rahman al-HUSAYN**
Min. of State	**Musaid bin Muhammad al-AYBAN**
Min. of State	**Muhammad bin abd al-Malik AL AL-SHAYKH**
Min. of State	**Mutalib bin Abdallah al-NAFISA**
Min. of State	**Assam bin Saad bin SAID**
Chmn., Supreme Ulama Council	**Abd al-Aziz bin Abdallah AL AL-SHAYKH**

Governor, Saudi Arabian Monetary Agency	**Fahd bin Abdallah al-MUBARAK**
Ambassador to the US	**Adil al-Ahmad al-JUBAYR**
Permanent Representative to the UN, New York	**Abdallah bin Yahya al-MUALLAMI**

Flag description:

green, a traditional color in Islamic flags, with the Shahada or Muslim creed in large white Arabic script (translated as "There is no god but God; Muhammad is the Messenger of God") above a white horizontal saber (the tip points to the hoist side); design dates to the early twentieth century and is closely associated with the Al Saud family which established the kingdom in 1932; the flag is manufactured with differing obverse and reverse sides so that the Shahada reads - and the sword points - correctly from right to left on both sides

note: the only national flag to display an inscription as its principal design; one of only

three national flags that differ on their obverse
and reverse sides; the others are Moldova and
Paraguay

National symbol(s):

palm tree surmounting two crossed swords

National anthem:

name: "Aash Al Maleek" (Long Live Our
Beloved King)

lyrics/music: Ibrahim KHAFAJI/Abdul Rahman
al-KHATEEB

note: music adopted 1947, lyrics adopted 1984

Chapter 5: Economy

Economy - overview:

Saudi Arabia has an oil-based economy with
strong government controls over major
economic activities. It possesses about 16% of
the world's proven petroleum reserves, ranks as
the largest exporter of petroleum, and plays a
leading role in OPEC. The petroleum sector
accounts for roughly 80% of budget revenues,
45% of GDP, and 90% of export earnings. Saudi
Arabia is encouraging the growth of the private

sector in order to diversify its economy and to employ more Saudi nationals. Diversification efforts are focusing on power generation, telecommunications, natural gas exploration, and petrochemical sectors. Over 6 million foreign workers play an important role in the Saudi economy, particularly in the oil and service sectors, while Riyadh is struggling to reduce unemployment among its own nationals. Saudi officials are particularly focused on employing its large youth population, which generally lacks the education and technical skills the private sector needs. In 2014 the Kingdom ran its first budget deficit since 2009, and faces budget deficits for the foreseeable future because it requires an oil price greater than $100 per barrel to balance its budget. Although the Kingdom can finance high deficits for several years by drawing down its considerable foreign assets or borrowing, it probably will begin to reduce capital spending if oil prices stay low throughout the next year.

GDP (purchasing power parity):

$1.616 trillion (2014 est.)

country comparison to the world: 15

$1.56 trillion (2013 est.)

$1.519 trillion (2012 est.)

note: data are in 2014 US dollars

GDP (official exchange rate):

$777.9 billion (2014 est.)

GDP - real growth rate:

3.6% (2014 est.)

country comparison to the world: 79

2.7% (2013 est.)

5.8% (2012 est.)

GDP - per capita (PPP):

$52,800 (2014 est.)

country comparison to the world: 20

$52,000 (2013 est.)

$52,000 (2012 est.)

note: data are in 2013 US dollars

GDP - composition by sector:

agriculture: 2%

industry: 59.7%

services: 38.3% (2014 est.)

Labor force:

11.22 million

country comparison to the world: 51

note: about 80% of the labor force is non-national (2014 est.)

Labor force - by occupation:

agriculture: 6.7%

industry: 21.4%

services: 71.9% (2005 est.)

Unemployment rate:

11.2% (2014 est.)

country comparison to the world: 122

11.6% (2013 est.)

note: data are for Saudi males only (local bank estimates; some estimates range as high as 25%)

Investment (gross fixed):

24.9% of GDP (2014 est.)

Budget:

revenues: $278.9 billion

expenditures: $293.3 billion (2014 est.)

Taxes and other revenues:

35.9% of GDP (2014 est.)

country comparison to the world: 56

Budget surplus (+) or deficit (-):

-1.9% of GDP (2014 est.)

country comparison to the world: 81

Public debt:

1.6% of GDP (2014 est.)

country comparison to the world: 164

2.7% of GDP (2013 est.)

Inflation rate (consumer prices):

2.9% (2014 est.)

3.5% (2013 est.)

Central bank discount rate:

2.5% (31 December 2008)

country comparison to the world: 126

Commercial bank prime lending rate:

6.8% (31 December 2014 est.)

country comparison to the world: 126

7.2% (31 December 2013 est.)

Stock of narrow money:

$301.1 billion (31 December 2014 est.)

country comparison to the world: 126

$266.8 billion (31 December 2013 est.)

Stock of broad money:

$461.1 billion (31 December 2014 est.)

country comparison to the world: 26

$412 billion (31 December 2013 est.)

Stock of domestic credit:

$-38.16 billion (31 December 2014 est.)

country comparison to the world: 190

$-58.7 billion (31 December 2013 est.)

Market value of publicly traded shares:

$373.4 billion (31 December 2012)

country comparison to the world: 26

$338.9 billion (31 December 2011)

$353.4 billion (31 December 2010)

Agriculture - products:

wheat, barley, tomatoes, melons, dates, citrus; mutton, chickens, eggs, milk

Industries:

crude oil production, petroleum refining, basic petrochemicals, ammonia, industrial gases, sodium hydroxide (caustic soda), cement, fertilizer, plastics, metals, commercial ship repair, commercial aircraft repair, construction

Industrial production growth rate:

3.6% (2014 est.)

country comparison to the world: 81

Current account balance:

$108.7 billion (2014 est.)

country comparison to the world: 3

$134.3 billion (2013 est.)

Exports:

$359.4 billion (2014 est.)

country comparison to the world: 18

$377 billion (2013 est.)

Exports - commodities:

petroleum and petroleum products 90% (2012 est.)

Exports - partners:

China 13.9%, US 13.6%, Japan 13%, South Korea 9.8%, India 9.5% (2013)

Imports:

$162.2 billion (2014 est.)

country comparison to the world: 31

$152.7 billion (2013 est.)

Imports - commodities:

machinery and equipment, foodstuffs, chemicals, motor vehicles, textiles

Imports - partners:

US 13.1%, china 12.9%, India 8.1%, Germany 7.4%, South Korea 6.1%, Japan 4.7% (2013)

Reserves of foreign exchange and gold:

$756.1 billion (31 December 2014 est.)

country comparison to the world: 4

$725.7 billion (31 December 2013 est.)

Debt - external:

$164.3 billion (31 December 2014 est.)

country comparison to the world: 36

$152 billion (31 December 2013 est.)

Stock of direct foreign investment - at home:

$242.1 billion (31 December 2014 est.)

country comparison to the world: 25

$232.3 billion (31 December 2013 est.)

Stock of direct foreign investment - abroad:

$31.51 billion (31 December 2014 est.)

country comparison to the world: 45

$27.06 billion (31 December 2013 est.)

Exchange rates:

Saudi riyals (SAR) per US dollar -

3.75 (2014 est.)

3.75 (2013 est.)

3.75 (2012 est.)

3.75 (2011 est.)

3.75 (2010 est.)

Fiscal year:

calendar year

Chapter 6: Energy

Electricity - production:

235.1 billion kWh (2011 est.)

country comparison to the world: 18

Electricity - consumption:

211.6 billion kWh (2011 est.)

country comparison to the world: 19

Electricity - exports:

0 kWh (2013 est.)

country comparison to the world: 190

Electricity - imports:

0 kWh (2010 est.)

country comparison to the world: 126

Electricity - installed generating capacity:

51.15 million kW (2011 est.)

country comparison to the world: 20

Electricity - from fossil fuels:

100% of total installed capacity (2011 est.)

country comparison to the world: 30

Electricity - from nuclear fuels:

0% of total installed capacity (2011 est.)

country comparison to the world: 172

Electricity - from hydroelectric plants:

0% of total installed capacity (2011 est.)

country comparison to the world: 194

Electricity - from other renewable sources:

0% of total installed capacity (2011 est.)

country comparison to the world: 120

Crude oil - production:

11.59 million bbl/day (2013 est.)

country comparison to the world: 1

Crude oil - proved reserves:

268.4 billion bbl (1 January 2014 est.)

country comparison to the world: 2

Refined petroleum products - production:

1.935 million bbl/day (2010 est.)

country comparison to the world: 10

Refined petroleum products - consumption:

2.925 million bbl/day (2013 est.)

country comparison to the world: 8

Refined petroleum products - exports:

1.471 million bbl/day (2013 est.)

country comparison to the world: 5

Refined petroleum products - imports:

196,700 bbl/day (2010 est.)

country comparison to the world: 26

Natural gas - production:

103 billion cu m (2013 est.)

country comparison to the world: 9

Natural gas - consumption:

103 billion cu m (2013 est.)

country comparison to the world: 9

Natural gas - exports:

0 cu m (2011 est.)

country comparison to the world: 142

Natural gas - imports:

0 cu m (2012 est.)

country comparison to the world: 124

Natural gas - proved reserves:

8.235 trillion cu m (1 January 2014 est.)

country comparison to the world: 5

Carbon dioxide emissions from consumption of energy:

582.7 million Mt (2012 est.)

Chapter 7: Communications

Telephones - main lines in use:

4.8 million (2012)

country comparison to the world: 31

Telephones - mobile cellular:

53 million (2012)

country comparison to the world: 26

Telephone system:

general assessment: modern system including a combination of extensive microwave radio relays, coaxial cables, and fiber-optic cables

domestic: mobile-cellular subscribership has been increasing rapidly

international: country code - 966; landing point for the international submarine cable Fiber-Optic Link Around the Globe (FLAG) and for both the SEA-ME-WE-3 and SEA-ME-WE-4 submarine cable networks providing connectivity to Asia, Middle East, Europe, and US; microwave radio relay to Bahrain, Jordan, Kuwait, Qatar, UAE, Yemen, and Sudan; coaxial cable to Kuwait and Jordan; satellite earth stations - 5 Intelsat (3 Atlantic Ocean and 2 Indian Ocean), 1 Arabsat, and 1 Inmarsat (Indian Ocean region)

Broadcast media:

broadcast media are state-controlled; state-run TV operates 4 networks; Saudi Arabia is a major market for pan-Arab satellite TV broadcasters; state-run radio operates several networks; multiple international broadcasters are available (2007)

Internet country code:

.sa

Internet hosts:

145,941 (2012)

country comparison to the world: 79

Internet users:

9.774 million (2009)

country comparison to the world: 29

Chapter 8: Transportation

Airports:

214 (2013)

country comparison to the world: 26

Airports - with paved runways:

total: 82

over 3,047 m: 33

2,438 to 3,047 m: 16

1,524 to 2,437 m: 27

914 to 1,523 m: 2

under 914 m: 4 (2013)

Airports - with unpaved runways:

total: 132

2,438 to 3,047 m: 7

1,524 to 2,437 m: 72

914 to 1,523 m: 37

under 914 m: 16 (2013)

Heliports:

10 (2013)

Pipelines:

condensate 209 km; gas 2,940 km; liquid
petroleum gas 1,183 km; oil 5,117 km; refined
products 1,151 km (2013)

Railways:

 total: 1,378 km

 country comparison to the world: 81

 standard gauge: 1,378 km 1.435-m gauge (with branch lines and sidings) (2008)

Roadways:

 total: 221,372 km

 country comparison to the world: 22

 paved: 47,529 km (includes 3,891 km of expressways)

 unpaved: 173,843 km (2006)

Merchant marine:

 total: 72

 country comparison to the world: 61

 by type: cargo 1, chemical tanker 25, container 4, liquefied gas 2, passenger/cargo 10, petroleum tanker 20, refrigerated cargo 3, roll on/roll off 7

 foreign-owned: 15 (Egypt 1, Greece 4, Kuwait 4, UAE 6)

 registered in other countries: 55 (Bahamas 16, Dominica 2, Liberia 20, Malta 2, Norway 3, Panama 11, Tanzania 1) (2010)

Ports and terminals:

Ad Dammam, Al Jubayl, Jeddah, Yanbu al Bahr

Chapter 9: Military

Military branches:

Ministry of Defense and Aviation Forces: Royal Saudi Land Forces, Royal Saudi Naval Forces (includes Marine Forces and Special Forces), Royal Saudi Air Force (Al-Quwwat al-Jawwiya al-Malakiya as-Sa'udiya), Royal Saudi Air Defense Forces, Royal Saudi Strategic Rocket Forces, Saudi Arabian National Guard (SANG) (2015)

Military service age and obligation:

17 is the legal minimum age for voluntary military service; no conscription (2012)

Manpower available for military service:

males age 16-49: 8,644,522

females age 16-49: 6,601,985 (2010 est.)

Manpower fit for military service:

males age 16-49: 7,365,624

females age 16-49: 5,677,819 (2010 est.)

Manpower reaching militarily significant age annually:

male: 261,105

female: 244,763 (2010 est.)

Military expenditures:

7.98% of GDP (2012)

<u>country comparison to the world</u>: 4

7.25% of GDP (2011)

Chapter 10: Transnational Issues

Disputes - international:

Saudi Arabia has reinforced its concrete-filled security barrier along sections of the now fully demarcated border with Yemen to stem illegal cross-border activities; Kuwait and Saudi Arabia continue discussions on a maritime boundary with Iran; Saudi Arabia claims Egyptian-administered islands of Tiran and Sanafir

Refugees and internally displaced persons:

stateless persons: 70,000 (2013); note – thousands of biduns (stateless Arabs) are descendants of nomadic tribes who were not officially registered when national borders were established, while others migrated to Saudi Arabia in search of jobs; some have temporary identification cards that must be renewed every five years, but their rights remain restricted; most Palestinians have only legal resident status; some naturalized Yemenis were made stateless after being stripped of their passports when Yemen backed Iraq in its invasion of Kuwait in 1990; Saudi women cannot pass their citizenship on to their children, so if they marry a non-national, their children risk statelessness

Trafficking in persons:

current situation: Saudi Arabia is a destination country for men and women subjected to forced labor and to a much lesser extent, forced prostitution; many men and women from Central Asia, the Middle East, and Africa who voluntarily travel to saudi Arabia as domestic servants or low-skiled laborers subsequently face conditions of involuntary servitude, including nonpayment, withholding of passports, restriction of movement, food deprivation, and abuse; some migrant workers are forced to work indefinitely beyond the term of their contract because their employers will not grant them a required exit visa; foreign domestic workers are particularly vulnerable because of their isolation in private homes; women, primarily from Asian and African coutnries, are believed to be forced into prostitution in Saudi Arabia, while other foreign women were reportedly kidnapped and forced into prostitution after running away from abusive employers; Yemeni, Nigerian, Pakistani,

Afghan, Chadian, and Sudanese children were subjected to forced labor as beggars and street vendors in Saudi Arabia, facilitated by criminal gangs

tier rating: Tier 3 - Saudi Arabia does not fully comply with the minimum standards for the elimination of trafficking and is not making significant efforts to do so; in 2013, the government did not report prosecuting or convicting any trafficking offenders and identified and referred fewer victims to protection services than in the previous reporting period; the sponsorship system, including the exit visa requirement, continues to restrict the freedom of movement of migrant workers and to hamper the ability of victims to pursue legal cases against their employers; the withholding of workers' passports remains widespread because legislation prohibiting the practice was not enforced; officials continue to arrest, detain, deport, and sometimes prosecute trafficking victims for unlawful acts committed as a direct result of being trafficked (2014)

Illicit drugs:
> death penalty for traffickers; improving anti-money-laundering legislation and enforcement

Other Key Facts™

Titles

Key Facts on Pakistan

Key Facts on Saudi Arabia

Key Facts on Cyprus

Key Facts on Iran

Key Facts on Afghanistan

Key Facts on Iraq

Key Facts on Indonesia

Key Facts on South Korea

All Key Facts™ Titles are

Available at

www.Amazon.com

THE

INTERNATIONALIST®

2015

www.internationalist.com